D1079404

A line-up of motor cabs in Knightsbridge in 1907. The leading cab is a French-built Sorex, unusual in having solid tyres. Behind the cabs is one of the sixty-four cabmen's shelters which were to be found all over London at that time.

THE LONDON TAXI

Nick Georgano

Shire Publications Ltd

CONTENTS

Published in 2000 by Shire Publications Ltd, Cromwell House, Church Street, Princes Risborough, Buckinghamshire HP27 9AA, UK. Website: www.shirebooks.co.uk
Copyright © 1985 by Nick Georgano. First published 1985. Second edition 2000. Shire Album 150. ISBN 0 7478 0436 2.

British Library Cataloguing in Publication Data available.

Printed in Great Britain by CIT Printing Services Ltd, Press Buildings, Merlins Bridge, Haverfordwest, Pembrokeshire SA61 1XF.

COVER: *A 1929 Morris Commercial G type International Taxicab, from a contemporary catalogue.*

BELOW: *One of the few surviving cabmen's shelters is in Brompton Road, nicknamed 'The Bell and Horns' after a long defunct public house. The first shelter was put up in 1874, in order to give cabbies a place for food, drink and rest other than in public houses. One of the strictest rules of the shelter was that no alcohol should be served, as Victorian cabmen were 'of mostly intemperate habits' according to Henry Mayhew's famous survey 'London Labour and the London Poor' (1851). Although various philanthropists paid for the shelters most were built to a standard pattern of solid oak painted dark green and resembling Victorian summerhouses. They used to be decorated with geraniums hanging in baskets from the eaves, but this pleasant custom seems largely to have been abandoned. Many were destroyed during the Second World War, including the famous 'Junior Turf Club' in Piccadilly, which attracted socialites and Guards officers during its heyday from the 1890s to the early 1920s. Others have disappeared in road-widening schemes, or because there was insufficient money to keep them in good repair.*

Contrasting shapes of recent London cabs – two FX4s followed by a TX1 with more rounded lines.

INTRODUCTION

London is unique among the world's cities in having a purpose-designed taxicab which has evolved over the years, but always within very strict limitations laid down by the Public Carriage Office. These have sometimes resulted in London taxis being held back from the mainstream of car development, in matters such as overall height and the adoption of front-wheel brakes, but they are nevertheless among the safest and most comfortable hire vehicles in the world. Anyone who has had to squeeze into a Citroën in Paris or a Plymouth in New York will vouch for this! Admittedly Americans have been able to enjoy a purpose-built cab in the shape of the Checker, but this is now out of production.

Londoners were first able to hail public vehicles in about 1620 when a certain Captain Baily bought four coaches, equipped his drivers with suitable livery and set them to ply for hire in the Strand. They soon attracted others, and within a few years at least a hundred were operating in London, causing severe congestion in the narrow streets. They were called hackney coaches, from the French *hacquenée*, meaning a strong horse hired out for journeys: a coach pulled by such a horse was fairly obviously a *coche à hacquenée*.

Numbers of hackney coaches rose rapidly, reaching seven hundred by 1694 and more than a thousand in 1768. By the nineteenth century the hackney had fallen into disrepute, and two new forms of transport appeared, the cab (from French *cabriolet de place*) and the four-wheeler or 'growler'. Cabs were always two-seaters and the best-known were the hansom cabs used from 1835 onwards. At first they were thought to be rather daring, for use only by the young and adventurous, and even in 1900 it was said that 'there are still some old ladies who will on no account enter a hansom, and shake their heads sorrowfully when they see their granddaughters doing so'. Growlers were slower and more respectable, as well as being essential if heavy luggage was to be carried. Hence they were to be found outside all the main railway stations and continued to ply their trade up to about 1930.

The growth in London's population and wealth in Victorian times was reflected by the number of cabs. In 1855 there were 2700 licensed cabs; five years later this figure had risen to 4300, while by December 1903 the total was 11,404, made up of 7499 hansoms and 3905 growlers. This amount has never been exceeded since, for the arrival of the motor cab saw a drop in overall numbers. If fewer cab drivers were employed, at least they had a better income, for sometimes a hansom cab driver might spend most of the day on the rank, and from 1899 they were forbidden to 'crawl' in search of customers, as they caused too much congestion in streets such as Piccadilly.

3

ABOVE: *Side view of a Bersey electric cab. This one is of the second pattern, with body made by the Gloucester Railway Carriage and Waggon Company. Note the vertical steering column and wheel, twenty-two turns of which were needed to move the front wheels from lock to lock.*

BELOW: *A Bersey cab at the London Electrical Cab Company's charging station in Lambeth. The cabs had forty batteries of 80 volts each, and charging took up to twelve hours.*

A 1905 Rational cab with 10/12 horsepower horizontal two-cylinder engine and two-speed epicyclic gearbox. At first the Rationals were fitted with solid rubber tyres, but in 1906 they changed to Palmer pneumatics, as seen here. The London Motor Cab Company of Chelsea ran a fleet of thirteen Rationals, keeping them until 1909.

MR BERSEY'S ELECTRIC CAB

The first motor vehicles to be used for hire were Benz cars, two of which plied for hire in Stuttgart in the spring of 1896, followed by a French-built Benz which operated in Paris in the autumn of the same year. Purpose-built electric cabs appeared in Philadelphia late in 1896 and arrived in New York in January 1897. London was not far behind, for in August 1897 twelve electric cabs began to operate from premises in Juxon Street, Lambeth.

The London Electrical Cab Company Limited was formed at the end of 1896, with share capital of £150,000 and the sponsorship of several prominent men in the transport world. These included H. R. Paterson, a director of Carter, Paterson and Company Limited, the well known goods carriers, the Hon Reginald Brougham, who was descended from the Lord Brougham who gave his name to a

four-wheeled coach in 1840, H. H. Mulliner, the coachbuilder, the Hon Evelyn Ellis, who was a pioneer motorist and director of the Great Horseless Carriage Company, and J. H. Mace, director of the Daimler Motor Company Limited. The cabs were designed by an electrical engineer, Walter C. Bersey, who gave his name to them. They had 3½ horsepower Lundell-type electric motors, which gave a speed of 9 miles per hour (14.5 km/h), and the batteries were sufficient for a range of 30 miles (48 km) between charges. This prevented drivers accepting long journeys, especially towards the end of the day, but it also provided a good excuse for those who felt they would not easily find a return fare. One passenger hired an electric cab to take him from Oxford Circus to Hampstead, but after travelling for a short distance it stopped. 'The electric power's gone,' said the driver. The passenger was obliged to get out, pay his fare and find other means of transport to Hampstead, whereupon he saw the cab proceeding merrily back to Oxford Street, its electric power miraculously restored.

The Bersey cabs seated two passengers, with the driver on a box ahead of them, and resembled horseless growlers. They had electric lights both inside and out, though the former were thought to be a mixed blessing. The author of *Omnibuses and Cabs*, H. C. Moore, said: 'they were, perhaps, a little too brilliantly illuminated for the comfort of people of a bashful disposition . . .'

By the end of 1897 there were twenty-five Bersey cabs running in London, and a further fifty were added to the fleet in 1898. At first they were well received by press and public ('This electrical Pegasus is very pleasant, quiet and smooth', said the *Daily News*), though the cab proprietors were worried that they would be forced to buy large numbers of these expensive new vehicles, and that the more skilled men needed to drive them would expect higher wages. However, the popularity of the electric cabs was short-lived: after six months' use they began to vibrate and rattle, and the battery box slid about and knocked against the floor of the cab. In April 1898 a new model appeared, built by the Gloucester Railway Carriage and Wag-

gon Company, with larger batteries giving a speed of 12 mph (19 km/h), and the body was mounted on springs which separated it from the motor and batteries, thus eliminating vibration. However, the novelty of the electric cab was wearing off: hirings were fewer, and the cost of batteries and tyre replacement proved much greater than the directors had anticipated. The company lost £6207 on the first twenty months of trading and decided to turn more to private hire work, which would be less strenuous than plying on the streets and would avoid the need for licensing by Scotland Yard.

A number of Bersey cabs continued to ply for hire, being rented from the company by drivers. The original figure was 6 shillings per day, but this was found to be uneconomic and was increased to 12s 2¼d a day, which considerably dampened the drivers' enthusiasm. In August 1899 the London Electrical Cab Company was liquidated; not a lot of money was realised as the specialised equipment was of little use to anyone else, and no one wanted to take over the business as a going concern. A few of the cabs were operated by private owners for nine months longer, but by June 1900 the last of these had been taken off the streets. Of the seventy-five Bersey cabs made only one is known to survive, in the National Motor Museum at Beaulieu, Hampshire.

EDWARDIAN MOTOR CABS

After the end of the Bersey era, the hansoms and growlers had the London cab trade to themselves for more than three years. Then, in December 1903, the first petrol cab arrived on the streets in the shape of a French-built Prunel 12 horsepower two-cylinder chassis with a two-passenger hansom-type body built by the old-established coachbuilders Henry Whitlock and Company of Holland Gate. Two others followed, and in May 1904 they were the first motor cabs to be licensed by the Metropolitan Police Office at Scotland Yard. At the end of 1904 there were still only the three Prunels running in London, but the following year several companies began

running cabs, and nineteen were in use by the end of 1905.

They were of diverse design, including the flat-twin Rational with central driving position, and the three-cylinder Vauxhall, whose driver was perched high up behind the passengers like the traditional hansom driver. A variety of makes followed over the next three years, mostly derived from small passenger car chassis. These included the Ford Model B, of which only five went into service, and the French-built Herald and Sorex. The Automobile Cab Company, which operated the Fords, originally ordered two hundred, but Ford's London manager, Percival Perry, had doubts about the

The 1905 Vauxhall motor hansom, of which three were operated by the Metropolitan Motor Cab Company of South Kensington. They were apparently popular with drivers, despite their exposed position, but most passengers found them alarming to ride in. 'Even to hardened motorists, the apparent rushing straight into danger without being able to see that the driver is doing anything to avert it must be at times disconcerting', said 'The Commercial Motor'.

soundness of the company and refused to sanction such a large order. His caution was justified, because the Automobile Cab Company was out of business by 1910. Meanwhile they ordered no fewer than forty Sorexes, the largest single order for motor cabs at that time, but whether these were ever paid for in full is not known.

The number of cabs licensed for use in London rose from nineteen at the end of 1905 to ninety-six a year later, and during 1906 the Public Carriage Office at Scotland Yard decided that they should issue construction and licensing regulations for motor cabs, as they had done for horse cabs since 1869. These laid down strict rules about the dimensions of chassis and body, and the quality of upholstery and appointments ('The cushions of seats . . . to be covered with leather, cloth of good quality . . . and not stuffed with hay, straw, seaweed or whalebone shavings').

A maximum turning circle of 25 feet (7.62 m) was laid down, which still applies to London cabs today, but apart from this the cab chassis and body did not have to differ greatly from the small town car of the day. This led to a host of manufacturers submitting cabs to the Public Carriage Office, hoping to share in the lucrative market which seemed to be imminent. Between 1905 and 1914 at least forty-five British and foreign manufacturers had cab designs licensed, compared with twelve between 1920 and 1930, and only four between 1930 and 1940.

As so often happens with a new invention, a few manufacturers soon cornered the market, and many of the forty-five were built only in small numbers, if at all. The most successful was Renault, who received an initial order for five hundred of their 8/9 horsepower two-cylinder cabs from the General Cab Company early in

ABOVE: *An early example of the famous Renault two-cylinder taxicab, of which several thousand went into service between 1907 and 1914. They all had two-cylinder engines and some were still in service in 1930, by which time they were quite outdated and attracted a lot of unfavourable comment.*

LEFT: *An Electromobile cab of 1908, driven by a single 8 horsepower motor powered by a forty-five cell battery. Twenty of these cabs, which were intended to replace the growlers for heavy luggage work, were put into service and ten were still to be seen on a rank in Gillingham Street, Victoria, in 1920.*

8

The curious Pullcar of 1906, powered by a 12/14 horsepower two-cylinder Fafnir engine driving the front wheels by chains. It was intended as an avant-train attachment to be fitted to horse-drawn cabs or delivery vans, hence the solid tyres on the rear wheels, although the front wheels have pneumatics. The Pullcar was licensed by Scotland Yard, who must have approved of its 20 foot (6 m) turning circle, but few went into service.

1907. This was the largest order for any kind of motor vehicle at that time, and before the end of the year a further six hundred went into service. Other manufacturers who enjoyed large orders were Richard Brasier of Paris, whose Unic cabs in two-cylinder and, later, four-cylinder form were used in large numbers up to the 1930s; Fiat, who had at least four hundred four-cylinder cabs on the streets; Darracq; Belsize; and Wolseley-Siddeley. Most cabs were of conventional design, with two or four-cylinder engines, three-speed gearboxes and shaft drive to the rear axle. There were exceptions, such as the front-wheel drive Pullcar, the Dawfield-Phillips with engine under the floorboards and single-chain final drive, and the Adams-Hewitt, which had a single horizontal cylinder and pedal operated two-speed epicyclic gearbox, but none of these was made in any numbers. Up to about 1910 motor cabs had seated two passengers only, but thereafter the four-seater became usual, with two occasional seats facing to the rear. There was also an electric cab, the Electromobile, whose chassis was made by Greenwood and Batley of Leeds, and body by the Gloucester Carriage and Waggon works, which had bodied the Bersey electrics ten years earlier. The Electromobile Taxicab Company was formed in 1908 to operate them, and it was planned that the fleet would number five hundred, but not more than twenty went into service. They were expensive to buy and, as always, batteries were a constant expense as well as limiting their range.

The arrival of the Renault and Unic cabs brought about a dramatic jump in the numbers of motor cabs, from 723 in 1907 to 2805 a year later. By 1910 motor cabs outnumbered horse cabs by 6397 to 4724, and in 1914 the figures were 7260 and 1391 respectively. The hansom cab suffered most, and there were only 232 registered when war broke out in August 1914. Second-hand hansoms fetched no more than one pound each, and nearly all were broken up, though one found its way to the London Museum in May 1912. The growler lasted longer because of its good luggage capacity and also because

9

ABOVE: *One of the less well known car makes was the Thames, a product of the Thames Ironworks, Shipbuilding and Engineering Company Limited, which had factories at Greenwich and Millwall. This 12 horsepower model of 1908 had a two-cylinder engine, metal cone clutch and worm-driven rear axle.*

BELOW: *A 16/20 horsepower Scottish-built Argyll cab, made in 1906. This was an unusual design in which the driver sat above the four-cylinder engine. The layout gave a useful amount of body space for a short wheelbase, but access to the engine was awkward, a serious drawback when they needed frequent attention. The steering and gearchange linkages were also complicated. Other makes to follow this design briefly included Humber and Lotis.*

ABOVE: *Taxicabs outside the now demolished arch at Euston station. The cab turning into the road is a 12/14 horsepower Unic, while those waiting at the right of the picture are another Unic and a Vinot, both French makes. The registration letters LF indicate a date of 1912 for the cabs, though the photograph may have been taken a year or two later.*

BELOW: *A 10/12 horsepower Humber cab of about 1908. The sign in the window of the house reads 'Motor car for hire. Terms moderate' indicating that the driver is a private owner. Such men were relatively rare early in the twentieth century when the purchase price of £500 or so was beyond most would-be taxi drivers.*

ABOVE: *A quartet of early Unic cabs, dating from 1908. These had 10/12 horsepower two-cylinder engines but were later replaced by larger models with 12/14 horsepower four-cylinder engines and roofs for the drivers. With small modifications the 12/14 was made up to the mid 1920s. Unics were sold by Mann and Overton Limited who later took on the agency for Austin taxicabs; they estimate that they have provided about 75 per cent of all London cabs.*

BELOW: *A 10 horsepower Napier cab of 1910 in Piccadilly Circus. In those days traffic was allowed to circulate around the statue of Eros in both directions. Note the white sidewall tyres and the driver's smart summer coat.*

motor cabs were not allowed into the main railway termini until 1910. This was because the railway companies would have had to pay higher insurance premiums if 'explosive machines' were allowed on to their premises.

Today everyone speaks of hailing a 'taxi', but this term did not come into use until 1907, when taximeters were first fitted to motor cabs. A meter to measure mileage and time was a German invention, first used on cabs in Berlin, Paris and other continental cities in the 1890s.

A few London hansoms were fitted with meters in 1899, but they were not widely adopted until the advent of the motor cabs. They were made compulsory on the latter in 1907, and many owners of growlers and hansoms adopted them in order to show that they were charging an honest fare. The charge for a motor cab was 8d per mile, compared with 6d for a horse cab. This led to a popular music hall song entitled 'The Taximeter Car' with the refrain 'You can do it in style for eightpence a mile'.

THE NINETEEN TWENTIES

The First World War brought chaos to the London cab trade, with a break-up of the large fleets. At the end of the war many cabs were off the road and many returning ex-servicemen were unable to afford to buy them. Only about one third of the 7260 taxicabs operating in 1914 were on the road in 1919. However, the hire-purchase companies came to the rescue, and the owner driver was soon able to buy a second-hand two-cylinder Renault for £200, or £180 if he could make an outright payment.

In May 1919 the first post-war taxicab was announced, from an unexpected source. William Beardmore and Company Limited was a very large Scottish engineering concern, with interests in shipbuilding and aero engines, as well as the manufacture of Arrol-Johnston and Beardmore private cars. Their taxicab was purpose-built for the trade, unlike nearly all the pre-war designs, which had been more or less based on passenger cars. It had a 2409 cc four-cylinder engine with detachable head and five-bearing crankshaft, leather cone clutch and four-speed gearbox. The frame was dropped halfway along, in order to give a reasonably low entrance and yet still comply with Scotland Yard regulations which stipulated a ground clearance of 10 inches (254 mm). Although built in Scotland, it had been designed after lengthy consultation with London cab operators and drivers, and from 1923 onwards Beardmore Motors Limited (a wholly owned subsidiary of William Beardmore and Company Limited) kept careful records

of all points noted at the service depots and incorporated these in future designs. The Mark I of 1919 was replaced by the only slightly modified Mark II in 1923 and this was made until the completely revised Mark III or 'Hyper' appeared in 1929. Beardmore rapidly became a familiar name among taxi drivers, in provincial cities as well as in London.

Soon other manufacturers followed Beardmore's lead in building specifically for the London cab trade. These included Fiat, whose 1846 cc four-cylinder engine was inherited from the pre-war Tipo Zero private car but was mounted in a cab chassis with the necessary turning circle and ground clearance. In 1923 another famous continental company, Citroën, brought out their taxi. This had the 11.4 horsepower 1450 cc engine from the B2 car, in a chassis swept up over the rear axle. Typical of the kind of modifications necessary to comply with the strict police regulations was the Citroën's steering. The drop arm was located inside the frame instead of outside, and the pull-and-push rod was taken obliquely over the spring and connected to the stub axle, instead of lying more or less parallel with the frame.

The Citroën cab was bought in considerable numbers by the Brixton-based London General Cab Company, one of the few large operating concerns still in business. In 1929 they brought out their own Citroën-based cab, using the current 1629 cc 13/30 horsepower engine, radiator and three-speed gearbox in a chassis designed and built at their works.

ABOVE: *A 1923 Beardmore Mark II, generally similar to the Mark I of 1919 but incorporating many minor improvements resulting from four years' experience by owners and drivers. This cab has a three-quarter landaulette body, with a small window or 'quarter light' between the main window and the landaulette hood.*

BELOW: *The chassis of a Mark II Beardmore, showing the dropped frame which provided a lower entrance level, despite the mandatory 10 inch (254 mm) ground clearance.*

A 1927 Beardmore Mark II (left) with one of the two-seater cabs which never plied for hire, a 10/20 horsepower Berliet. The latter's registration number, 058LB, is a London trade plate.

The fabric body was also built at Brixton and had high-quality upholstery, safety glass and a Burovox communication system between passenger and driver. This consisted of a push-button operated microphone located at the passenger's side so that he did not need to lean forward and tap the glass division. Because of more relaxed regulations the London General Citroën was markedly lower than the earlier models.

A curious phenomenon of the 1920s was the two-seater cab. Since about 1910 all London cabs had seated four passengers, but this was not so in many provincial cities, where light cars such as the

A Fiat 1T cab with an 1846cc four-cylinder engine that gave it a top speed of 37 mph (60 km/h). It is seen here on the Fiat stand at the 1921 Commercial Motor Show at Olympia.

Morris Cowley and Clyno carried two-passenger taxi bodies. In 1925 the Home Secretary, Sir William Joynson-Hicks, appointed a committee to hear evidence on the question of two-seater cabs for London. The chief argument in favour was that the conventional taxi could not be run profitably at less than one shilling per mile, which was the current charge, yet this was too high for many people and was keeping potential cab users away. A two-seater, having a lower initial cost, as well as lower running expenses, could be run at 9d a mile and still make a profit for the owner.

The cab trade was unanimously against the two-seater, arguing that there were already too many taxis on the streets working for only three hours a day: more cabs would only make matters worse. An Owner Drivers' League was formed, which argued that the two-seater cab would drive its members back to working for big companies, and the Motor Cab Trade Protection Society and the Transport and General Workers' Union were other bodies who opposed any reduction in fares.

The committee eventually came out cautiously in favour of the two-seater (in a splendidly roundabout way, they said that 'It is not desirable that the Home Secretary should make an order which would prohibit the licensing of a vehicle which complies with Scotland Yard requirements on the sole grounds that it is constructed to carry fewer than four passengers') and Joynson-Hicks licensed them in April 1926. The press called these new cabs Jixis, after the Home Secretary's nickname, 'Jix'. However, only prototypes appeared, and a year later Jix had a change of heart, rescinding the Two-Seater Order in return for an agreed reduction in fares from 1 shilling to 9d per mile.

Three companies built prototypes for the boom that never happened: White, Holmes and Company of Hammersmith, who made a small 9.8 horsepower four-cylinder car, called the KRC, on which the two-seater cab was to have been based; Trojan of Kingston upon Thames, whose unconventional two-stroke engined car had become very popular; and the large French company Berliet, whose 10/20 horsepower chassis was widely used for taxicab work in their native Lyons and other French cities.

This 1925 Citroën cab, conforming to Scotland Yard's original regulations, can be compared with that on the opposite page.

The London General Cab Company's version of the Citroën cab, made in 1929 after Scotland Yard's restrictions on cabs had been revised.

THE NINETEEN THIRTIES

In 1927 a committee set up to enquire into the high cost of taxicabs found that lack of competition between manufacturers was the main reason. This in turn was due to the specialised nature of the design, so that few manufacturers thought it worthwhile to bring out a new vehicle of which they could not hope to sell more than a thousand a year, at best. Therefore the committee made a number of recommendations aimed at bringing the taxicab closer to the ordinary private car. The most important recommendations were that the ground clearance minimum be reduced from 10 to 7 inches (254 to 178 mm), and that the turning circle be increased from 25 to 40 feet (7.6 to 12.2 m). Superintendent Claro at Scotland Yard agreed with all recommendations but the turning circle, and the reduced ground clearance led to a spate of new taxicabs appearing between 1928 and 1930.

As well as the London General Citroën already mentioned, new models included the Beardmore Mark III Hyper, a revised Unic which was assembled in London, and two new cabs from major manufacturers, the Morris Commercial International and the Austin Twelve Four. The Beardmore Hyper had a smaller engine of 1954 cc, which gave it a horsepower rating of 12.8 instead of 15.9 for its predecessor. This was a useful change in the days when tax was paid on a sliding scale of £1 per horsepower. It was also 6 inches (152 mm) lower than the Mark II and had four-wheel brakes, the first of their kind on a London taxicab. Before 1929 they had been forbidden by the very conservative Public Carriage Office, on the grounds that sudden stops might cause accidents, and that better brakes would encourage cabbies to drive faster than was necessary or desirable. This was despite the fact that by 1929 practically every private car made incorporated front-wheel brakes.

The London-assembled Unic was not a great success, being less reliable than the older models, and fewer than a hundred were made in three years, but the Morris Commercial started a line of taxicabs which the company was to make up to the Second World War. It had a 2½ litre 15.9 horsepower four-cylinder engine, which was a modified version of that used in the Morris Empire Oxford private car, four-speed gearbox and overhead worm-drive rear axle. The first hundred or so Interna-

ABOVE: *One of the first Austin cabs, a 1930 model with three-quarter landaulette coachwork by Strachan.*

BELOW: *In order to avoid the problem of the passenger door hitting pedestrians, W. Gowan from Cape Town devised a cab in which the door slid across the frame. This was first seen on a Morris Commercial International in 1929, and in 1933 about twenty Austins, of which this is one, were fitted with a modified form of the 'Cape' body by Arthur Mulliner of Northampton.*

A 1937 Morris Commercial G2SW Junior Six single landaulette cab. This model was also available as a three-quarter landaulette. Note the generous space for luggage next to the driver, necessary in the days when many people travelled with heavy cabin trunks.

tionals had weak rear axle casings which frequently cracked, harming the new model's reputation, but this was rectified on subsequent cabs. Because of regulations prevailing when the International came out in January 1929, it lacked front-wheel brakes and a side screen for the driver, but both these features were included in the next Morris Commercial cab, the G2 of 1932. This had a smaller engine of 1.8 litres, borrowed from the Morris Oxford car, and lower lines than the International. This was joined in 1935 by the G2S Junior Six with 1.9 litre six-cylinder engine, one of the few sixes ever used in the London taxicab trade. The final Morris Commercial taxi, which took the company up to the outbreak of war, was the G2SW, similar in appearance to the G2S but with an overhead valve 1.8 litre engine as used in the Morris Fourteen-Six Series III. Morris never played a major part in the cab scene, and the total number made between 1929 and 1939 was 2125, compared with 5850 Austins registered in London alone and over a shorter period.

The arrival of the Austin and its rapid dominance of the London cab trade was the most important development of the 1930s. It came about because Mann and Overton's staple business of supplying Unic cabs was dwindling by the late 1920s, as the French machines were both old-fashioned and expensive. They looked around for a new make to sell and noticed the Austin Heavy Twelve Four, a rugged and reliable 1861 cc side-valve chassis, of which thousands had been made since its introduction in 1921. Cab versions had been running in provincial cities such as Manchester and Liverpool, but their turning circle was too great for them to be allowed in London. However, Mann and Overton persuaded Austin to rectify this, and in June 1930 the first Austin cab for twenty years (a few had plied in about 1910) appeared on London's streets. It had a landaulette body by Dyer and Holton of Brixton. Most Austin cabs were bodied by London firms which were chosen by Mann and Overton for their quality. The best known were Jones of Westbourne Grove, Strachan of Acton, and, from out of town, Vincents of Reading. Other coachbuilders included the Chelsea Carriage Company, Christopher Dodson of Chelsea, Ricketts

Two typical Austin LLs of the mid 1930s. Above: a single landaulette by Strachan. Below: a three-quarter landaulette by Jones. The latter has the typical Jones 'fishtail' body, swept out at the rear and enclosing the spare wheel.

of Euston and two firms which combined coachbuilding with operating fleets of cabs, Birch Brothers of Kentish Town, and Goode and Cooper of Brixton. All these firms made proper coachbuilt bodies in metal on ash frames, and nearly all their cabs were landaulettes, with the rear portion openable in fine weather. They were quite expensive, costing around £400 in the early 1930s, when a Heavy Twelve Four private car could be had for under £300. A curiosity of the time was the 'Chinese Austin', a hybrid built by the London General Cab Company which carried a body taken off a superannuated Citroën cab and mounted on the new Austin chassis. A total of 196 were made and sold mainly to owner drivers, or 'mushes', as they were nicknamed.

The Austin taxi underwent several changes during the 1930s. For 1933 synchromesh was provided on third and top gear, giving rise to the name Twin Top (TT), and in 1934 the roof line was lowered by some 6 inches (152 mm), owing to a worm-drive rear axle. Even though the floor was also lowered, there was no propeller shaft 'hump' as this was, and still is, forbidden by Scotland Yard

Two examples of the 1938-9 Austin cab, nicknamed by drivers the 'Flash Lot'. Above: a standard Jones landaulette. Below: a rarer three-quarter landaulette by Strachan.

regulations. The new cab was known as the LL or Low Loader, so the previous Austins were retrospectively named HLs (High Loaders), though also known by cabbies as Grand Pianos or Upright Grands.

In mid 1938 came the final development of the pre-war Austin cab. This had the same Twelve Four engine and artillery wheels as the LL, but the lines were updated with the narrow, sloping radiator grille found on Austin cars, horizontal bonnet louvres and skirted mudguards. Conservative cabbies nicknamed it the 'Flash Lot', and it was made

up to the outbreak of war in September 1939. A few already completed cabs were delivered up to January 1940, and about four hundred chassis were acquired by the army, for whom they were fitted with light truck bodies and used for general duties and driving instruction.

Beardmore continued with taxicab production in the 1930s, but at the end of 1933 production was transferred from Scotland to a new factory at Hendon, in north-west London. At the same time the Hyper was replaced by a cheaper cab called the Paramount, powered by a 1944 cc four-cylinder engine made by

ABOVE: *The last pre-war Beardmore, the Paramount Mark VI of 1938, fitted with a three-quarter landaulette body.*

BELOW: *A Strachan bodied 1935 Austin LL with ladder, blackout markings on the wings and masked headlamps. It is still in the London General Cab Company's livery, indicating that the photo was taken early in the Second World War. By 1940 the AFS cabs had been painted in grey London Fire Brigade livery.*

Commer, the truck-building division of the Rootes Group. Beardmore built their own bodies, in four styles, single landaulette, three-quarter landaulette, four-light saloon and six-light saloon. The Paramounts continued the mark numbering of the earlier Beardmores, so the 1934 model was the Mark IV, replaced in 1936 by the longer-wheelbase Mark V, and at the end of 1937 came the Mark VI, with synchromesh on all four speeds. Beardmores were more expensive than Austins, at £485 for a Mark VI three-quarter landaulette, and far fewer were sold.

THE SECOND WORLD WAR

Taxicabs and their drivers played an important part in the defence of London between 1939 and 1945. When war was declared their strength stood at 6690 motor cabs, eight growlers and one hansom. The fate of the horse cabs is not known (the last hansom driver, presumably the same one, turned in his licence in 1947) but of the motor cabs 2452 were requisitioned for war work. Most of these were used for towing trailer-mounted fire pumps, with ladders on their roofs, and hoses in the luggage compartment. The crews were all cab drivers, whose knowledge of London's short cuts often enabled them to get to the scene of a blaze before the larger fire engines. All the drivers were attached to the Auxiliary Fire Service of the London Fire Brigade and wore fireman's uniform with steel helmets.

About two thousand cabs were used by the AFS, and four hundred were fitted with machine guns and employed on anti-paratroop patrol work. When the threat of invasion receded these were either added to the AFS fleet, which was constantly being depleted by enemy action, or returned to civilian use. Despite the heroic efforts of Mann and Overton to keep war-worn cabs on the road, in addition to devoting the bulk of their factory space to war production, many taxis were off the road because of lack of spare parts. Others had been destroyed in air raids, so that in 1945 there were fewer than three thousand cabs fit for use.

A 1947 Wolseley Oxford. The driver had just won a turkey in a cabbies' Christmas draw.

The six-light version of the Oxford, introduced in 1950 in reply to Austin's light and airy FX3. A similar model, with fourth door and bench front seat, was called the Hire Car and became popular with provincial taxi operators.

THE POST-WAR TAXICAB

Three makes catered for the London taxi trade in the 1950s, Austin, Beardmore and Wolseley. The Wolseley Oxford was the first to appear, and a prototype had been running throughout the war, covering nearly 100,000 miles (160,000 km). The Oxford was built at Wolseley's factory at Ward End, Birmingham, and had a 1.8 litre four-cylinder overhead valve engine, four-speed gearbox and a pressed steel limousine body. The landaulette of pre-war days had gone for ever, being too expensive to produce, though the Oxford did have some ash in the frame. The interior of the four-light body was rather dark, acceptable by pre-war standards, but in response to the lighter Austin FX3 Wolseley brought out a six-light cab in 1950. This body was also used on the private-hire car, which had a front door on the nearside, and a front seat in place of the luggage area.

Pre-war Morris Commercial cabs had been distributed by William Watson and Company of Grosvenor Road, London SW1, but after the war Mr Watson retired, and Beardmores became concessionaires for the Oxford. They had operated the prototype during the war, and as they did not immediately resume production of their own taxi it was an ideal solution. About eighteen hundred Oxfords were sold by Beardmores up to 1952, when the Austin-Nuffield merger put an end to the Oxford. There was not room for two taxicabs in the British Motor Corporation, and as Austin's FX3 was the more modern design the Oxford was dropped.

The FX3 appeared in June 1948 and was completely different from the pre-war Austin Twelve Four. The engine was an overhead-valve four of 2199 cc as used in the Austin Sixteen and later A70 Hampshire and Hereford saloons and developed 52 brake horsepower, subsequently increased to 56 brake horsepower. The all-steel body was by Carbodies Limited of Coventry, who have provided coachwork for London taxicabs ever

ABOVE: *Austin's popular FX3, of which 7267 were sold for service in London between 1948 and 1958. The FX3 was sold in chassis form as well, and a number were fitted with van bodies and used for the delivery of London newspapers.*

BELOW: *Many pre-war cabs were later used as student transport. This 1934 Beardmore Paramount IV carried the names of thirty-eight European cities when it was photographed in 1960, and it was also lettered 'New South Wales', though perhaps that was just wishful thinking.*

An early Beardmore Paramount Mark VII, photographed near Regent's Park in December 1954, the month when it was presented to the Public Carriage Office. Deliveries to the cab trade began in February 1955.

since. For the first time on a London cab the driver's compartment was fully enclosed, with a sliding window on his left. Another 'first' was an enclosed luggage compartment at the rear, in addition to the platform next to the driver.

Two very important innovations appeared on the FX3 during its ten-year life span, the diesel engine and automatic transmission. The small diesel engine was a boon to the cab trade, which had seen fuel prices rise by more than 80 per cent compared with pre-war days. The first such engine was made by the Standard Motor Company, a 2-litre four-cylinder unit adapted from that used in the Ferguson tractor. Birch Brothers offered a conversion for £325 including labour, and operators soon found that fuel costs could be cut by as much as 50 per cent. In September 1954 Austin brought out their own 2.2 litre diesel. The initial cost was £942, compared with £857 for a petrol-engined FX3, but most operators thought the extra worthwhile, and in 1955 Mann and Overton were selling nine diesels to every one petrol cab.

The diesel engine, combined with the abolition of Purchase Tax on cabs in the 1953 Budget led to greatly increased sales of new taxis. The long-serving pre-war Austins or Beardmores were retired at last, some to be driven by students all over Europe and as far afield as Australia. The last HLs went in 1951, and by 1955 there were virtually no pre-war cabs in London service.

Automatic transmission was not offered on the FX3 by the factory, but York Way Motors fitted eighteen of their cabs with Borg-Warner automatic gearboxes, and the experience gained on these led to their being standardised on the FX4 of 1958. The FX3 was the first London taxicab to be exported in any quantity. Foreign sales numbered about seven hundred, of which 250 went to Spain and the balance to Sweden, Denmark, Ireland, Iran and New Zealand. A few were tried in New York and San Francisco, but they were underpowered compared with the American cabs with 100 or more brake horsepower.

26

The Paramount Mark VII was the last London cab design to have an exposed platform for luggage, though a fourth door was added in 1965. Visible here is the drive to the meter and the strap for attaching luggage.

London's third post-war taxi was the new Beardmore, introduced in 1954 when the company no longer had Wolseley Oxfords to sell. The Paramount Mark VII was powered by a 1508 cc Ford Consul engine and gearbox and was the first London taxicab to have a steering column gearchange. The aluminium-panelled body was made for Beardmore by their neighbours in Hendon, Windovers Limited, who had made a lot of high-class coachwork on Rolls-Royce and Bentley chassis before the war. In 1958 a Perkins Four 99 diesel engine was offered as an alternative to the Ford Consul but was noisier and less popular than the Ford units. The Beardmore Mark VII was made in small numbers up to 1967, gaining a fourth door enclosing the luggage area in 1965. A Mark VIII replacement never got further than the design stage, and Beadmore disappeared from the cab scene after fifty years.

A Mark III Winchester of 1970. This Cortina-engined fibreglass cab was operated by W. H. Cook and Company, who offered a conversion from petrol to propane gas. They claimed that the £150 charge would be recouped in seven to eight months running.

The familiar shape of the Austin FX4 has been a symbol of London since 1958.

THE FX4 AND BEYOND

In September 1958 the FX3 was replaced by an all-new design, jointly developed by Austin and Carbodies. The FX4 had a full-width body without running boards, which made it seem much wider than its predecessor, though the actual increase was only 1 inch (25 mm). The body was also 4 inches (102 mm) longer, though the wheelbase was the same. The FX4 had coil independent front suspension, and the Borg-Warner automatic transmission tried out on the York Way Motors FX3 was standardised on the new cab. However, a manual synchromesh gearbox was made optional later, though relatively few were supplied. London cab drivers were and are still not prepared to put up with the extra strain of driving manual gearbox taxis despite the extra costs involved.

The FX3's 2178 cc diesel engine was continued, being joined in 1962 by the 2199 cc petrol engine used in the FX3. The latter was continued up to 1974 but sold only in small numbers. In 1970 eighty petrol FX4s were sold in London, compared with 1398 diesels. They were more likely to be bought by owner drivers than by fleet operators, as owner drivers tend to undertake longer journeys, when the higher speed of the petrol cab is important. A petrol-engined FX4 had a maxi-mum speed of 75 mph (120 km/h).

Two years before the petrol engine was dropped, the capacity of the diesel was enlarged to 2520 cc. Considering that it was in production from 1958 to 1997, the FX4 underwent very few other changes. Tinted glass in the rear window was replaced by clear glass in 1969, and the turn indicators were moved from the roof sides to the rear wings in 1970. In 1982 the BMC diesel engine was replaced by a 2.2 litre Land-Rover unit, but this was not very satisfactory and was replaced in 1985 by a 2.5 litre Land-Rover engine. This, in turn, gave way to a 2.7 litre Nissan diesel in 1987. At the same time the cabs were renamed Fairway, though the designation FX4 was still widely used. An automatic transmission became available with the Nissan engine in 1989 and was favoured by the majority of cabbies. Meanwhile Carbodies and distributors Mann & Overton had been incorporated in London Taxis International, a subsidiary of Manganese Bronze Holdings. Although the 1997 LTI Fairway looked superficially similar to the 1958 Austin FX4, only a single component, the driver's interior door handle, remained the same.

To assist foreign tourists, the traditional illuminated sign 'For hire' has given way

29

to 'Taxi', which is an international word. More than seventy-four thousand FX4s have been built, and they have been exported to many foreign countries, including Dubai, Saudi Arabia, Lebanon, Kuwait, Japan and the Falkland Islands, where the Governor has two as his official transport. In 1984 Carbodies made a sale to the USA at last, an agreement being signed with a Detroit company to supply five hundred cabs, with engines and transmissions being fitted in America. Several firms over the years have offered customised FX4s for private ownership; usually the modifications were confined to the interior, but Tickfords, the Milton Keynes coachbuilders, have offered a stretched FX4 with 16 inches (406 mm) added to the wheelbase and extra windows on each side, with plush upholstery and burr walnut interior. Optional extras include cocktail cabinets, computers, television or a boardroom table. A standard FX4 ready for the London cab trade cost £10,083.92 in 1985, but the basic Tickford model would cost over three times as much.

Only one other make of taxicab went into service to challenge the FX4 in the mid 1960s. This was the Winchester, made by a subsidiary of Westminster Motor Insurance and designed by a number of owner drivers. Its outstanding feature was a body completely made of fibreglass which was both light and rust-free. It incorporated an illuminated recessed step and was of striking appearance, with colouring in two tones of grey. It was powered by a Perkins Four 99 diesel engine, but this was soon replaced by a $1^1/2$ litre Ford Cortina petrol engine, which was quieter and more lively. This Mark II Winchester abandoned the dual-tone colouring for a traditional black, and this was followed on the restyled Mark III made from 1968 to 1972. Fewer than two hundred Winchesters were made; most were run by owner drivers, though some were operated by W. H. Cook and Company of Hammersmith.

In 1971 Metropolitan-Cammel-Weymann, the well-known builders of bus bodies and underground railway carriages, built two prototype taxicabs called the Metrocab, powered by a 1.8 litre Perkins diesel engine, with Ford Transit gearbox and transmission and fibreglass bodies. They were tested extensively by the London General Cab Company, but production did not get under way until 1987. They had several advantages over the FX4, including power steering and a collapsible steering column, disc brakes and wheelchair access, the last being later adopted on the FX4. A Series II Metrocab appeared in 1995 and a Series III in 1998. Styling was improved, and different seating configurations were available for five,

The London Taxis International TX1, introduced in October 1997. It is available with five-speed manual or three-speed automatic transmissions. The makers hope for international sales, especially to the United States and Japan.

six or even seven passengers. The engine is now a 2.5 litre Ford direct injection diesel. Metrocabs are made at Tamworth, Staffordshire, and are part of the Hooper Group, which includes the custom coach-builders Hooper & Company. By the end of 1996 4283 had been made. The Duke of Edinburgh has had three, the latest running exclusively on LPG.

Metrocab's rival is London Taxis International's TX1, the successor to the FX4/Fairway, which was introduced in October 1997. It had the same Nissan diesel engine as its predecessor, with more rounded body lines and many improvements for the comfort of both driver and passengers. These include greatly improved seating, air conditioning and in-car entertainment for the driver, and in the rear compartment there is a taller door and wider seat, an integral child's seat built into the central armrest, and a power point for mobile phones and laptop computers. Initial production of the TX1 was 60 per week, increasing to 70-80 in 1999.

Other experimental taxis have come and gone. Lucas Industries built an electric cab in 1975 and another in 1977, and Mitsubishi showed their MMT forward-control cab on a van chassis at the 1980 Motor Show. It won a prize in the coach-work section but got no further. It looks as if the traditional cab, still called a black cab though many now carry brightly coloured advertising, will be around for a long time yet. If the TX1 lasts as long as the FX4, its replacement will not be seen on London's streets before 2037!

The second version of the Lucas electric taxi, as demonstrated in 1977. It had the same carrying capacity as an FX4 but was more than 3 feet (1 m) shorter. A 50 brake horsepower CAV motor gave the Lucas a top speed of 55 mph (88.5 km/h) and a range of 70-80 miles (110-130 km).

FURTHER READING

Bobbit, Malcolm. *Taxi! The Story of the London Taxicab.* Veloce, 1998.
Buckland, Robert. *Share My Taxi.* Michael Joseph, 1968.
Georgano, G. N. *A History of the London Taxicab.* David & Charles, 1972.
Gilbey, Sir Walter. *Early Carriages and Roads.* Vinton, 1903.
Levinson, Maurice. *Taxi.* Secker & Warburg, 1963.
May, Trevor. *Gondolas and Growlers: the History of the London Horse Cab.* Alan Sutton, 1995.
May, Trevor. *Victorian and Edwardian Horse Cabs.* Shire, 1999.
Moore, H. C. *Omnibuses and Cabs.* Chapman & Hall, 1902.
Warren, Philip, and Linskey, Malcolm. *Taxicabs – A Photographic History.* Almark, 1976.

PLACES TO VISIT

Few London taxicabs are to be seen in museums, although quite a number survive in private ownership. Among museums which have one or more taxis are the following.

Museum of London, 150 London Wall, London EC2Y 5HN. Telephone: 020 7600 3699. Website: www.museumoflondon.org (Horse-drawn hansom cab.)

Myreton Motor Museum, Aberlady, East Lothian, Scotland EH32 0PZ. Telephone: 01875 870288. Beardmore Mark VII.

National Motor Museum, John Montagu Building, Beaulieu, Brockenhurst, Hampshire SO42 7ZN. Telephone: 01590 612345. Website: www.beaulieu.co.uk (1897 Bersey Electric, 1908 Unic 12/14 horse-power, 1997 LTI FX4R.)

Science Museum Large Object Store, D4 Hanger, Red Barn Gate, Wroughton, Swindon, Wiltshire SN4 9NS. Telephone: 01793 814466. Website: www.nmsi.ac.uk/wroughton (1922 Unic 12/14 horsepower.)

Privately owned London taxicabs can often be seen at vintage vehicle rallies throughout Great Britain, especially in the annual London to Brighton Run of the Historic Commercial Vehicle Society, which takes place on the first Sunday in May. The organisation for owners of these vehicles is the London Vintage Taxi Association, 51 Ferndale Crescent, Cowley, Uxbridge, Middlesex UB8 2AY. Taxis of all makes and years are catered for by the Vintage Taxi Club: B. A. Sockett (Honorary Treasurer), 30 Cenarth Drive, Cwmbach, Aberdare, Mid Glamorgan CF44 0NH.

ACKNOWLEDGEMENTS
With the exception of those listed below, all illustrations, including the front cover, are from the Photographic Library of the National Motor Museum. The photographs on pages 2, 3 and 32 are by Cadbury Lamb; those on pages 15 (lower), 16, 17, 21, 25 and 29 are from the author's collection. That on page 30 is by courtesy of London Taxis International.

A Series III Metrocab carrying Dial-a-cab radio circuit logo, photographed in Whitehall.